Original title:

Smoky Films Over the Fae Punt

Author: Kene Elistrand

ISBN HARDBACK: 978-1-80563-339-6

ISBN PAPERBACK: 978-1-80564-860-4

Surreal Dance in the Clouded Light

In twilight's embrace, shadows play,
Whispers of dreams drift away,
Clouds weave tales in the fading light,
A symphony born of day and night.

Figures twirl in a waltz so rare,
Each step ignites the evening air,
Colors bloom in a spectral trace,
Lost in the rhythm, time finds its place.

A shimmer glows where thoughts collide,
Mirrors reflect what hearts confide,
As laughter blooms like starry seeds,
The soul surrenders to its needs.

Soft echoes ring through the misty air,
Dancing on dreams, we travel where
Boundless laughter and silence meet,
A dance of shadows, bittersweet.

With every pulse, the night takes flight,
In surreal hues of clouded light,
We sway in rapture, lost in trance,
In the magic of this endless dance.

Veiled Horizons and Dreaming Stars

Beyond the veil where shadows roam,
Horizons beckon, calling us home,
Stars whisper secrets in muted tones,
Dreams intertwine in silvery moans.

A tapestry woven of night and day,
Each thread a wish that fades away,
Guided by starlight's gentle hand,
We journey forth to a distant land.

In the stillness, echoes softly gleam,
Chasing the shimmer of a wandering dream,
Time like a river flows through our sight,
Infused with the magic of fading light.

Veiled horizons stretch far and wide,
Where heartbeats linger, and hopes abide,
Each star a promise, bright and clear,
Illuminating paths we hold dear.

Embrace the stillness, let fears depart,
As we dance with shadows in the dark,
For in this realm, the unknown flows,
In veiled horizons, our spirit grows.

Magic Woven in Hazy Threads

In the heart of the night where mystics dwell,
Spells are spoken, casting an enchanting spell.
Silver sparks dance, tracing tales of old,
In shadows and whispers, the secrets unfold.

With every flicker, a story unwinds,
Of love and of loss, of fate that entwines.
Threads of moonlight weave through the air,
A tapestry rich, woven with care.

Listen closely, hear the silence speak,
Of journeys begun, of futures bleak.
Colors of magic, vivid and bright,
Guide wandering souls through the depths of the night.

Airy Threads of Forgotten Journeys

Through breezes that whisper of paths once tread,
Lies the soft echo of words left unsaid.
Veils of the past drape over the dawn,
In the hush of the morning, all worries are gone.

With every gust, memories unfold,
Stories of courage in the shadows of bold.
Threads of adventure in every breath,
Charting a course beyond life and death.

In twilight's embrace, dreams gently turn,
Lessons etched deep in the heart where they burn.
Carved by the winds of chance and choice,
Each thread a reminder, a beckoning voice.

Veiled Portents Beneath Twilight Skies

When twilight descends, the stars start to gleam,
A canvas of mystery, a midnight dream.
Veils of the cosmos, secrets concealed,
In shadows of starlight, the fate is revealed.

Whispers of prophecy drift on the breeze,
Calling the faithful, the brave, and the free.
Threads of assurance in darkness alight,
Guiding the wanderers through the long night.

In the hush of the heavens, silences sigh,
Promises linger as time passes by.
Each twinkle a story, each shade a muse,
In the dance of the cosmos, no soul can refuse.

Whispers of Sorrows in the Soft Haze

In the soft haze of morning, tears softly fall,
Echoing heartaches that silence enthrall.
Veils of emotion wrap tightly around,
Where shadows of sorrow in stillness are found.

With each breath of dawn comes a glimpse of the past,
Threads of remembrance link futures to last.
In the weeping of willows, stories arise,
Of love once so deep, now echoes and sighs.

Yet even in sadness, a beauty remains,
In the cycles of heartache, the joy and the pains.
For every soft whisper beneath skies so grey,
Holds echoes of promise, a brighter day.

Veils of Twilight in Enchanted Glades

In twilight's hush, the glades do sigh,
Beneath the boughs where secrets lie.
Whispers weave through branches high,
As shadows flirt with the night sky.

Glimmers dance on leaves aglow,
Where ancient rivers quietly flow.
Elven songs from thickets throw,
A gentle magic in the low.

Fireflies twinkle, soft and bright,
In realms where day fades into night.
Each heartbeat marked by pure delight,
Nature's arms hold dreams so tight.

With every step, the ferns now part,
A melody stirs within the heart.
In enchanted glades, the journey starts,
Elysian realms where no soul departs.

Tomorrow waits with silver wings,
Yet in the dark, the starlight sings.
In twilight's fold, a journey clings,
To magic's breath, our spirit springs.

Whispers of a Gossamer Dream

In realms where dreams take gentle flight,
Soft whispers drift like velvet night.
Gossamer threads weave paths of light,
A tapestry of stars so bright.

Silver winds through meadows sweep,
Cradling secrets the moon can keep.
Echoes tender, in silence deep,
Awake the wishes lost in sleep.

Fluttering hearts in dreams collide,
Embracing wonder, worlds to bide.
In slumber's arms, we softly glide,
On hopes and visions, time will ride.

With every breath, new realms arise,
Enchanting tales where magic lies.
In the folds of night, we memorize,
The wonder seen in slumber's eyes.

Awake, the dawn will surely call,
Yet while we dream, we stand so tall.
In gossamer dreams, we risk it all,
To dance on shadows, never fall.

Shadows Dance Among Hidden Glens

Where shadows dance in hidden glens,
The murmurs of the forest blend.
Trees bow low to ancient friends,
A secret world where magic mends.

Moonbeams slip through leaves that sway,
In twilight's arms, the spirits play.
Each gentle rustle dreams convey,
As night unveils its soft ballet.

A rush of wind, a whispered sigh,
In shadowed corners, spirits fly.
Beneath the stars, we dare to try,
To glimpse the beauty drawn nigh.

Around each bend, the stories twine,
In glens where hearts and fortunes shine.
A magic draft in every vine,
A timeless path, both yours and mine.

As dawn approaches, tales renew,
In shadows' dance, hope breaks anew.
Among the glens, the spirit flew,
With whispers soft, our journey grew.

Misty Reveries Beneath the Moonlight

In misty realms where shadows blend,
Under moonlight, night will send.
Canvas of dreams that never end,
Soft reveries we quietly tend.

Silver droplets kiss the ground,
With every step, a magic sound.
Whispers linger, love profound,
In moonlit hours, we are spellbound.

Lost in thoughts, the world around,
A melody where hearts are found.
In misty realms, dreams are unbound,
With every sigh, new hopes resound.

The night unfolds its secrets deep,
With every glance, the stars will leap.
In moonlight's glow, our wishes sweep,
To places where the heart can keep.

At break of dawn, the mist will part,
Yet in our souls, the night will start.
In misty reveries, we take heart,
To find the magic in every art.

Secrets Bound in Foggy Silhouettes

Beneath the veil where shadows creep,
Whispers of secrets softly seep.
In corners dim, where phantoms dwell,
Lost tales emerge, too dark to tell.

The moonlight dances on silver streams,
Illuminating hopes, unraveling dreams.
Yet in this twilight, hearts may ache,
For every promise holds a break.

Figures glide through shrouded mist,
Fingers trace where sorrows twist.
With every secret bound by time,
The haunting echoes slowly rhyme.

Ancient trees entwine their roots,
With stories woven deep in boots.
A tapestry of fables spun,
Each sighing leaf, a tale begun.

So when you walk through fog's embrace,
Listen closely; you'll find your place.
For in the quiet, truths reside,
And shadows dance on the moonlit tide.

Lurking Dreams of the Enchanted

In twilight shades where faeries play,
Lurking dreams begin to sway.
Beneath the boughs of ancient trees,
Magic stirs upon the breeze.

Glistening dew on petals bright,
Whispers secrets of the night.
In hidden glades where shadows blend,
Hope and wonder softly mend.

Each fluttered wing, a story spun,
Of battles fought and victories won.
In every heart, a wild desire,
To seek the flames of the inner fire.

But beware the darkness that conceals,
For lurking dreams can oft reveal.
A truth that cuts with sharpened edge,
An invitation to a wily pledge.

So close your eyes and take a chance,
Join in the enchanted dance.
In realms of magic, lose your fear,
As the lurking dreams draw near.

Chimeras in an Ocean of Mist

In waves of fog that cling so tight,
Chimeras rise in ghostly light.
Figures formed from fleeting dreams,
Drifting by on silver streams.

A siren's song, a tempest's wail,
Echoes of a whispered tale.
Each shadow calls with secrets deep,
In oceanic realms where phantoms creep.

With every breath, the mist unfolds,
Unseen forces, brave and bold.
Beyond the depths where visions play,
Chimeras dance; they guide the way.

Yet heed the warnings in the air,
For in the mist, dangers flare.
With every turn, the truth may bend,
In this maze where nightmares blend.

So sail your ship on ebbing tides,
Through veils where timeless magic hides.
Embrace the journey, trust the quest,
For in this mist, we find our rest.

Faery Laments in Obscured Horizons

In dusk's embrace, the faeries cry,
Underneath a shadowed sky.
Their ballads weave through time and space,
Echoes of love lost without trace.

Upon the hills where spirits roam,
A longing song, a wistful home.
In whispers soft, their tales unfold,
Of passions fierce, of wishes bold.

Through scattered dreams on breezes light,
Faery laments fill the night.
Each note a memory, sweet and sad,
A bridge to paths in twilight clad.

Though silhouettes may surely fade,
The heart remembers what was laid.
In every tear, a spark ignites,
With hopes reborn in starry nights.

So listen close to echoes faint,
Of faery hearts and earthly paint.
For in the shadows, they reside,
Where laments of love and loss abide.

Enchantment Caught in Twilight's Grasp

In shadows where the whispers creep,
The stars awaken from their sleep.
A flicker here, a shimmer there,
Magic dances in the air.

The trees, adorned in silken glow,
Breathe secrets only night can know.
Each petal holds a story wise,
Beneath the watchful, twinkling skies.

The moon casts spells with silver light,
Illuminating realms of night.
In twilight's grasp, we dare to dream,
Where nothing's ever as it seems.

With every breath, the magic swells,
In every heart, a tale compels.
We're caught within this mystic song,
Where shadows whisper, right and wrong.

So linger 'neath this spellbound sky,
Let echoes of enchantment fly.
For in the dusk, we all can see,
The world unfolds, wild and free.

Portraits of the Unseen in Hazy Realities

In the mist, where silence reigns,
Lives the art of hidden pains.
Portraits hung on walls of air,
Stories linger, rich and rare.

Brushstrokes soft, like whispered breath,
Capture moments born from death.
A fleeting glance, a sorrowed sigh,
The unseen truth that you can't buy.

Fragments dance in hazy light,
Filling shadows, banishing night.
Each visage tells a tale untold,
Of hearts both fragile, brave, and bold.

Colors blend, then fade away,
Echoes of what words can't say.
Here lies the canvas of the soul,
Where dreams and nightmares take a toll.

So wander through this spectral place,
Embrace the mystery that you face.
For in the fog, the heart can see,
The portraits of our history.

Legends Beneath a Misty Canopy

Beneath the boughs of ancient trees,
Legends whisper on the breeze.
Tales of magic, lost in time,
Echo softly, pure as rhyme.

In the twilight woods, they roam,
Every spirit finds a home.
With every rustle, secrets blend,
In leafy shadows, tales transcend.

The forest holds its breath in awe,
As moonlight casts a gentle law.
In silver beams, our hearts ignite,
Guided by the whispers of night.

Creatures stir in twilight's glow,
Where dreams and legends ebb and flow.
Each heartbeat marks the path we tread,
With ancient wisdom overhead.

So gather 'round and take your stand,
In this enchanted, timeless land.
For from the mist will rise the voice,
Of legends past that still rejoice.

Ripples of Prayer in Gossamer Fog

In the dawn, when silence breaks,
A thousand thoughts, like water makes.
Ripples spread across the lake,
Softly woven, lives awake.

The fog, a shroud that cloaks the day,
Whispers secrets in its play.
Each breath a prayer released to skies,
With hopes and dreams that never die.

Underneath the silver veil,
Echoes of our hearts set sail.
As shadows dance behind the haze,
We find the light in love's embrace.

Each droplet carries tales of yore,
Stories rich in peace and lore.
The world awakens with each prayer,
In soft embrace, we lose our care.

So let the ripples guide your way,
In gossamer fog, where spirits sway.
For in the stillness, find your truth,
In whispers soft, reclaim your youth.

Fantasies Resting on Shady Shores

In the twilight glow, dreams take flight,
Where whispers dance in the soft moonlight.
Mermaids sing of tales untold,
On sandy banks where magic unfolds.

Shadows flicker beneath leafy trees,
As breezes carry the scent of the seas.
Each shell holds a secret, a wish, a prayer,
A promise woven in the salty air.

Stars shimmer bright in the heavens above,
A tapestry woven of purest love.
The tide reveals treasures from afar,
As night surrenders to dawn's first star.

Gentle waves lap at the shores of time,
Echoing softly a haunting rhyme.
The world spins slowly, yet dreams race on,
Where the heart finds solace until the dawn.

Laughter echoes, a child's delight,
As fantasies linger, cloaked in the night.
In this realm where our hopes entwine,
On shady shores, all seems divine.

Illusions of Time Within the Mist

Veils of fog whisper tales of old,
In the stillness, their secrets unfold.
Time dances slowly, a waltz in gray,
As echoes of yesterdays softly sway.

Memories linger like shadows cast,
In the embrace of the mist from the past.
Each fleeting moment, a treasure small,
Captured in silence, a ghostly call.

Footsteps are muffled on paths unseen,
Where time's gentle fingers weave in between.
A labyrinth winding, both twisted and vast,
In the hallways of dreams, we are ever fast.

The clock ticks on with a soft, muted chime,
Marking the rhythm of endless time.
In this ephemeral dance, we find our way,
Within the mist, where illusions play.

As dawn breaks through with a timid light,
Illusions of time dissolve in the sight.
Yet, the echoes remain, tender and sweet,
In the heart of the day, where memories meet.

The Realm Beyond the Veil

Behind the veil where shadows dwell,
Lies a kingdom woven with tales to tell.
Starlit paths lead to wonders rare,
Adventures call from the midnight air.

Whispers beckon from fables untold,
Of knights and dragons, both brave and bold.
In the heart of the forest, magic stirs,
As the world turns vibrant with sound and purrs.

Time is a tapestry, rich and wide,
In this enchanted land where dreams abide.
Every corner hides a secret sparse,
In the tender glow of the moonlit farce.

With each glimpse through the silken threads,
Unfold the lore of the spirits that led.
A dance of colors, a symphony true,
In the realm beyond, where wishes come due.

So wander forth, be fearless and wild,
Let your heart guide you, like a child.
In the depth of the night, magic unveils,
The beauty that rests in the realm beyond veils.

Sable Whispers from the Enchanted Realm

In the shadows, secrets softly sigh,
As twilight spreads its cloak in the sky.
Sable whispers curl in the dusky air,
Tales of enchantment linger everywhere.

Through the thickets, where the wild things roam,
Beasts of legend find their hidden home.
Every rustle speaks of a story bold,
In this realm where the forgotten is gold.

Moonbeams cast flickers on pathways unseen,
Guiding the dreamers where fairies convene.
In the hush of night, wonder takes flight,
As magic unfurls in the soft silver light.

Watch closely, dear heart, for shadows will dance,
In the glimmering glow of fate's sweet chance.
Sable whispers will cradle your dreams,
In a world woven with silvery seams.

So listen, intently to soft melodies,
Let them carry you across timeless seas.
In the heart of the night, where enchantments gleam,
Sable whispers weave the fabric of dream.

Elfin Echoes in Hazy Realms

In misty glades where shadows play,
Elves weave tales that drift away.
With laughter soft like silver bells,
They sing of secrets, ancient spells.

Beneath the boughs of ancient trees,
They dance with grace upon the breeze.
Whispers swirl in twilight's glow,
In these realms where few dare go.

Every spark, a wish afloat,
In lacey dreams, their voices coat.
Through glimmering lights, the night is spun,
An echo of the woodland's fun.

With stars above, the night ignites,
In these quiet, enchanted nights.
They beckon softly, visions near,
In the heart of mystery, no fear.

An elfin hymn, a timeless tune,
Wanders slowly, touching the moon.
Between the realms of dream and facts,
Lies a joy where wonder acts.

Secrets Woven in Starlit Canopies

In twilight's grasp, where shadows sigh,
Secrets bloom under the starlit sky.
Threads of silver, soft and bright,
Knit the dreams that dance with night.

Through canopies where whispers dwell,
Each leaf a tale, a magic spell.
The moonlight drapes a gentle veil,
Enchanting stories none can stale.

Woven tight in nature's quilt,
A tapestry of dreams is built.
The nightingale sings sweet and low,
As secrets rise, like rivers flow.

Glimmers flicker like distant charms,
Calling forth the magic's arms.
In this realm of hushed delights,
Woven whispers become long nights.

Dancing stars in silent flight,
Guide the heart through endless night.
In every rustle, every sigh,
Lie the secrets that never die.

Ethereal Glimmers of a Forgotten Tale

In shadows deep, where memories fade,
Ethereal glimmers of dreams were laid.
Under the stars, whispers take flight,
Painting tales within the night.

Vows of the lost, sweetly resound,
In every heartbeat, hope is found.
Fading echoes of laughter's grace,
Time dances softly, leaving no trace.

Stories woven in moonlit seams,
Awaken the heart, revive the dreams.
In silver light, the past each day,
Spins a tale that will not sway.

Glimmers like dust from ages gone,
Remind us of where we belong.
Each gentle sigh, each pulse of light,
Breathes life into the quiet night.

A tapestry of lost desires,
In whispered words, fate conspires.
In every flicker, hope prevails,
Eternal echoes of hidden tales.

Wraiths of Light in Whispering Woods

In whispering woods where shadows roam,
Wraiths of light call the lost home.
With flickering forms that dance and sway,
They guide the hearts that drift astray.

Through sun-dappled glades, a shimmer bright,
Illuminates the depth of night.
Softly twinkling through leaf and bark,
These phantoms create their magic spark.

Their laughter echoes, soft and clear,
In songs that only the brave can hear.
Each glow a promise, each glide a chance,
Inviting souls to join the dance.

From twilight's cradle, they arise,
Chasing dreams beneath starry skies.
In every rustle, a tale unfolds,
Of bravery found and courage bold.

Wraiths of light guide the night's embrace,
Encasing the world in shimmering grace.
For in these woods, so wild and free,
Joy awakens, and spirits flee.

Traces of Magic Amidst the Haze

In whispers soft, a spark ignites,
Amidst the mist, where wonder lights.
A hidden door, a fleeting chance,
To dance with fate in moonlit trance.

The shadows weave a tale untold,
Of days gone by, of legends old.
A flicker bright, a hint of grace,
In corners dark, a warm embrace.

Dreams like starlight swirl and play,
In twilight's hush, they drift away.
But in that space, where silence clings,
The heart remembers, and magic sings.

The world awakens, softly spun,
With every breath, the morning's run.
In every leaf, a story sighs,
Of fading echoes, and wistful skies.

So chase the light through tangled wood,
Embrace the mystery, as one should.
For where the magic blurs the line,
A heart embarks on paths divine.

Fragments of Light in Obscured Pathways

Beneath the boughs, where shadows creep,
A fractured glow, in silence deep.
The pathway winds through veils of green,
In every step, enchantment seen.

A glint of dawn on dew-kissed grass,
Illuminates the moments pass.
The air is thick with tales unsaid,
Of dreams once lost, of hopes now fed.

Among the stones where secrets lie,
A whispered breeze begins to sigh.
The fragments bright, like scattered beads,
Will guide the heart where yearning leads.

Through tangled trees and ancient breezes,
The journey calls, as time still pleases.
With every turn, a spark anew,
Awaits the brave, the dreamers too.

And in the dusk, as light grows thin,
The fragments spark, and hope begins.
Amidst the fog, a vision clear,
Emerges free, as night draws near.

Elven Echoes Through Ethereal Clouds

In twilight's shimmer, soft and pale,
The elven song begins to sail.
Through whispered winds, a harmony,
That draws the heart to ancient trees.

The clouds, like dreams, they drift and sway,
In silver hues of dusk's array.
An echo calls from realms unseen,
Where time could pause, and hearts convene.

In twilight's grace, the secrets flow,
The moonlight dims, the shadows grow.
Each note released, a wish fulfilled,
In every heart, adventure thrilled.

Amongst the stars, where silence weaves,
The story dances, as each heart believes.
An elven whisper shared in flight,
Through endless skies, in boundless night.

So listen close, as shadows tread,
In every dream, where hope is fed.
For echoes linger, soft and true,
In ethereal realms, where all is new.

Veiled Visions Above the Moors

Above the moors, where spirits roam,
Veiled visions rise, a haunting poem.
In misty shrouds, the echoes sigh,
Of tales once lived, of love's goodbye.

The heather blooms in gentle sway,
As whispers waltz at end of day.
In twilight's hush, the shadows play,
A lullaby for hearts that stray.

Through every fog, the spirits weave,
In patterns strange, they take their leave.
But linger here, in twilight's care,
And find the magic resting there.

The moors hold secrets in their chest,
Where weary souls may find their rest.
In veiled visions, a guiding spark,
Illuminates paths through the dark.

So rise with dawn, embrace the light,
For dreams await beyond the night.
With every step, the world unfolds,
A tapestry of tales retold.

Ethereal Games in the Dappled Dark

In the woods where shadows play,
Dappled light begins to sway,
Whispers of a hidden spark,
Unfold secrets in the dark.

Pixies dance on silver beams,
Mischief woven into dreams,
Laughter echoes, light will fade,
Magic flits in night's parade.

Underneath the ancient trees,
Mysteries ride on the breeze,
Crickets sing their nightly tune,
While the stars become the moon.

Footsteps soft on leafy ground,
Every breath a gentle sound,
In this realm of quiet grace,
Time is lost in shadowed space.

Ethereal games played on leaves,
Where time weaves in webs of dreams,
Moments caught in twilight's art,
Entranced, we drift, heart to heart.

Haunting Whispers of the Twilight Vale

Within the vale where shadows cling,
Whispers of the past take wing,
Echoes of a haunted fate,
Ghostly tales reverberate.

Flickering lights on the water's edge,
Ancient vows made in a pledge,
Silhouettes in moonlight weave,
Memories that dare to leave.

In the stillness, time must yield,
Secrets in this magic field,
Gentle murmurs, soft and low,
Haunting where the wild winds blow.

Nature's pulse in twilight blurs,
Every breath a shiver stirs,
From the depths, a past revealed,
Show the scars the heart concealed.

Souls entwined in silver mist,
Truth and shadow coexists,
In this vale, we dare to dream,
Chasing echoes like a gleam.

Fables Adrift in Sable Mist

In the mist where fables breathe,
Stories wrapped in twilight's wreath,
Every sigh a tale untold,
Whispers of the brave and bold.

Characters drift like autumn leaves,
Bound by the magic that deceives,
Heroes rise and villains fall,
In this realm, where shadows call.

Beneath the stars, the night unfolds,
Ancient lore that softly molds,
From the legends softly spun,
Dreams awaken, one by one.

Sable mist, a cloak of time,
Hides the pathways, dimmed and climb,
Journeying through realms uncharted,
To find the dreams once dearly started.

Fables drift on winds of night,
In every shadow, there's a light,
As we wander, hand in hand,
In this space, together stand.

Twilight Mists that Ensnare the Heart

Twilight mists rise softly near,
Ensnaring hearts with whispered cheer,
Floating thoughts like petals fall,
Dancing to an ancient call.

Veils of dusk, they gently fold,
Secrets in their arms, they hold,
In the hush, our dreams ignite,
Painting all the world in light.

Amidst the whispers, echoes blend,
Promises that seem to mend,
In the twilight's calming sway,
Hope and love drift underlay.

Every sigh a vow, intent,
In the fading day, we're pent,
Wrapped in shadows, fear departs,
Entwined, forever, our hearts.

Twilight mists that softly share,
Magic woven everywhere,
In this realm, our spirits twine,
In the fading light, you're mine.

Chimeras of Light Beneath the Boughs

In twilight's glow, the shadows play,
Beneath the boughs where chimeras sway.
With whispers soft, they weave their spells,
In secret realms where magic dwells.

The fireflies blink like stars in flight,
Guided by dreams through the misty night.
A tapestry spun with threads of gold,
Holds tales of wonder, yet untold.

Through ancient trees, the voices rise,
Soft lullabies beneath starlit skies.
Each rustling leaf, a story shared,
Of hope and magic, gently bared.

With every sigh, the night unveils,
The secrets bound in ethereal trails.
Chimeras dance, their laughter bright,
Beneath the boughs in the fading light.

So linger here, where dreams take flight,
Embrace the magic, surrender the night.
For in this realm where shadows form,
The heart finds peace, the spirit warm.

Whispers in the Mist

The mist rolls in, a silken shroud,
Whispers calling from the crowd.
Secrets linger upon the breeze,
Voices echo through ancient trees.

With every step, the world transforms,
Into a dance where magic warms.
Soft echoes weave a haunting song,
Guiding souls where they belong.

The shadows shift as twilight falls,
And gentle dreams through silence crawl.
A tapestry of dusk unfolds,
With tales of love and legends old.

In hidden glens where spirits tread,
Each whisper speaks of what lies ahead.
Through misty paths, the heart will roam,
In every breath, a tale of home.

So heed the call, let visions rise,
The mist is where the magic lies.
Embrace the secrets held so tight,
And dance with shadows in the night.

Enchanted Shadows Dance

In moonlit glades where shadows twine,
The dance begins with a whispered line.
Underneath the starlit skies,
Enchanted spirits come alive.

They swirl and twirl on the velvety ground,
In rhythm with the night's soft sound.
Each flicker of light a fleeting glance,
As dreams take form in the merry dance.

With laughter bright, they take your hand,
A silent vow in this enchanted land.
Through winding paths of silver beams,
They lead you on through woven dreams.

The night is young, the magic true,
As shadows play in shades of blue.
With every step, let wonder rise,
In the heart of night beneath the skies.

So lose yourself where the shadows sing,
And feel the joy that darkness brings.
For in this dance, both wild and free,
The spirit soars, the heart will see.

Ethereal Veils of Twilight

In twilight's embrace, a softness grows,
Ethereal veils of twilight flows.
With whispers sweet like fireflies' glow,
They beckon softly, come and know.

Beneath the skies of deepening hue,
Where magic stirs and dreams come true.
Each moment wrapped in starlit lace,
Holds all the secrets time can't erase.

The air is thick with promise clear,
A world that whispers, "Come draw near."
In quiet corners, shadows dance,
Inviting hearts to take a chance.

The stars above, like sentinels bright,
Guide weary souls through the velvet night.
With every step, the shadows twine,
To weave a story that feels divine.

So linger longer, let shadows hold,
Their tender touch in twilight's fold.
For in this realm of dreams set free,
Ethereal veils unveil the key.

The Enchanted Orchestra of Shadows

In twilight's grasp, the shadows dance,
Their whispers weave a spellbound trance.
Notes of longing, soft and low,
As moonlit phantoms start to glow.

Strings of starlight, violins cry,
Underneath the velvet sky.
And as the night begins to swell,
The tales of dusk, they rise and tell.

Fingers brush on ancient wood,
Echoes sing where dreamers stood.
A harmony of lost desires,
Awakens deep within the fires.

Each haunting cacophony unfolds,
A symphony of stories told.
In shadows keen, our hearts take flight,
Enchanted songs illuminate the night.

So let the music drift and soar,
For in its embrace, we long for more.
In shadows soft, we'll lose our fears,
As the orchestra plays on through the years.

Echoes of Secrets Beneath Misty Vales

In valleys green, where silence sleeps,
The echoes hide, their secrets keep.
Beneath the mist, they softly creep,
To whisper tales where shadows weep.

Ancient oaks with branches bare,
Guard witnesses of dreams laid bare.
From every nook, a story bleeds,
In hushed tones, the heart now pleads.

With every rustle, a hint of lore,
Of spirits passed and lovers' war.
Through tangled paths, the secrets sigh,
Where twilight merges with the sky.

For every step upon the ground,
A tale awakens, lost and found.
In echoes soft, the past remains,
Resonant in the misty lanes.

So wander here, where shadows dwell,
Listen close, for all may tell.
In whispers cool, the history sways,
Among the secrets of these bays.

Fractured Tales in a Veil of Smoke

In flickering flames where shadows blend,
Fractured tales of start and end.
With colors bright, then faded dim,
A dance of echoes, wild and grim.

Each swirling wisp, a story lost,
Of dreams betrayed and love's great cost.
In smoky shrouds, our memories tie,
To remnants where the lost ones lie.

When night unfurls its dusky cloak,
The world stands still beneath the smoke.
And in the haze, the visions bloom,
Awakening long-forgotten gloom.

From dusky depths, a voice takes flight,
Unfolding secrets in the night.
With every breath, the tales unfold,
In whispered hints of truths retold.

So gather close, hear shadows sing,
Of fragile ties and yearning's sting.
In whispered realms, our fates entwine,
Within the smoke, our lives align.

Horizon Dwellers Beneath the Enigma

The horizon waits with bated breath,
For mysteries of life and death.
Dwellers roam where dreams ignite,
In realms between the day and night.

With spirits bold, the seekers tread,
Through paths unknown, the light they shed.
In shadows cast, the truths emerge,
As twilight calls, their hearts converge.

With every step, a star ignites,
In whispered tales of wondrous sights.
The enigma of the dawn unfolds,
With every secret softly told.

Across the skies, the colors play,
Unveiling wonders in the gray.
For those who dare to see beyond,
The horizon speaks, a silent bond.

So fear not, fellow dreamers' quest,
For in the unknown, we find our rest.
In the arms of evening's glow,
Forever dwellers, we shall know.

Crystal Veils of a Wandering Spirit

In realms where whispers softly glide,
A spirit weaves through shadows wide.
With crystal veils that shimmer bright,
She dances on the edge of night.

Her laughter echoes in the gleam,
A fleeting thought, a tender dream.
Through silvered woods, she twirls with grace,
And leaves behind a silken trace.

With every step, the stars do sigh,
Beneath the vast and endless sky.
In twilight's hush, her secrets swirl,
A wandering soul, a timeless girl.

Among the trees, she finds her way,
Through night's embrace, where shadows play.
The crystal veils, a soft allure,
In their embrace, one feels so pure.

She calls to those who seek the light,
To join her in this mystic flight.
With heart and mind in tune, we chase,
The magic found in her embrace.

Wraiths of Memory in Enchanted Nights

When night unfolds its velvet cloak,
In stillness, silent wraiths invoke.
They weave through time, both near and far,
And whisper tales beneath the stars.

From dreams forgotten, shadows rise,
In haunted echoes, soft goodbyes.
They dance upon the edge of sleep,
In silent realms where memories seep.

They flicker in the candle's glow,
As stories from the past bestow.
With every sigh, they gently glide,
Through heart and mind, they bide their side.

In enchanted nights, they call our name,
These wraiths of memory, ever the same.
With glistening eyes, they seek to share,
The moments lost, the joys laid bare.

So listen close, as shadows sing,
To every heart, the echoes bring.
In the dance of dreams, we find the key,
To a world alive with mystic glee.

Chimera's Lullaby Under Fading Stars

Beneath the canopy of night,
A chimera sings, a wondrous sight.
Her voice, a softness in the gloom,
Rests gentle as the roses bloom.

With shimmering scales and wings of grace,
She weaves a lullaby in this place.
Around her, dreams begin to rise,
Illuminating the starlit skies.

The tales of old, she softly spins,
With every note, the magic begins.
In twilight's hush, and shadows play,
She lulls the world to dream away.

Her melody flows like a soothing stream,
Embracing us in a loving dream.
In harmony, the stars do sway,
As chimera's song lights up the way.

So let your heart be filled with peace,
As night and wonder gently cease.
Under fading stars, we softly lay,
To the chimera's lullaby, we drift away.

Celestial Sighs in the Silvery Mist

In misty folds where silence dwells,
The whispers of the heavens tell.
Celestial sighs entwined with light,
Guide lost souls through the starry night.

Each breath a promise, soft and deep,
In silvery mist, the dreams we keep.
They dance upon the cool night air,
With secret hopes, and hearts laid bare.

The constellations weave their tales,
As moonlight bathes the tranquil trails.
With every pulse of gentle stars,
We share their wisdom, near and far.

The world unfolds in quiet grace,
In this ethereal, timeless space.
Celestial sighs become our guide,
As we step forth with hearts open wide.

In the embrace of night's delight,
Each whispered breath ignites the light.
So let us drift in dreams tonight,
In silvery mist, till morning bright.

Enchantment's Lament in Hazy Nights

In the hush of twilight's grace,
Whispers echo, soft embrace.
Stars are dancing, shadows play,
Lost in dreams that fade away.

Moonlight weaves a silver thread,
Tales of magic, softly spread.
Through the mist, the spirits sigh,
Beneath a canvas darkened sky.

Echoes of a bygone spell,
With every heartache, secrets swell.
Where the memories linger still,
In the valleys, hopes fulfill.

Time unfolds its gentle wings,
Carrying the weight of things.
Softly now, the shadows fade,
In the light where dreams are laid.

In the gloom, a spark ignites,
Guided by the night's delights.
With every heartbeat, truths arise,
In enchantment's tender lies.

Sirens of Smoke in Fairyland Glimmers

In a realm where shadows flow,
Sirens sing, a haunting show.
Whispers lost in velvet air,
Innocence stripped bare with care.

Winds of amber, copper gleam,
Pigments swirl, crafting dream.
With every ribbon twirled and spun,
Secrets beckon, one by one.

Veils of fog conceal the night,
Inviting echoes, soft and light.
Magic drips from every tree,
Woven deep, our destiny.

Flickering lights in shades of blue,
Dance and beckon, ever true.
Lost in beauty, spirits soar,
Through the paths they once adored.

In the realm of dreams, I wait,
With every heartbeat, feel the fate.
Sirens whisper, secrets blend,
Where the fairy tales transcend.

The Glistening Chill of Gossamer Nights

Underneath a shivering sky,
Gossamer threads weave and tie.
Chill of stillness paints the air,
Dreams shimmer bright, yet beware.

Frosted whispers touch the ground,
In this silence, magic found.
With every breath, the night unfolds,
Ancient secrets to be told.

Stars above twinkle with grace,
Guiding hearts to another place.
In the glistening dreams we chase,
Each moment finds its rightful space.

Hushed reflections, silver streams,
Flowing gently through our dreams.
In the night, a cautious light,
Softly calls the lost to flight.

Underneath the moon's embrace,
Wanderers find their sacred place.
Gossamer nights will gently weave,
The tales that we hope to believe.

Illusions Danced on Flickering Breezes

In the twilight's brittle breath,
Illusions dance, whisper of death.
Flickering shadows, light and dark,
Symbols weave a fateful arc.

Through the glades, a laughter sings,
Carried on the softest wings.
In the dusk where wishes bloom,
Chasing dreams beyond the gloom.

Breezes flutter, secrets flow,
Through the leaves, the stories grow.
In the heart of every gleam,
Flickering hopes weave through the dream.

While the world beneath us sleeps,
In our hearts, the magic leaps.
Illusions spark and intertwine,
In the dance where dreams align.

With each heartbeat, shadows cast,
Fleeting moments, captured fast.
As we twirl on blissful air,
Illusions fade, we're unaware.

Mirage of Gossamer Dreams

In the weave of twilight's thread,
Whispers dance on the soft winds,
Illusions shimmer just ahead,
Where the laughter of starlight begins.

Through the mist where shadows play,
A path unfolds in silver haze,
Each step a journey far away,
In dreams that twirl and set ablaze.

Gossamer hopes like fireflies,
Flutter near the heart's command,
Glancing up at gravity's lies,
As wishes spill like grains of sand.

Fleeting moments, soft as sighs,
Glimmers flicker, then they wane,
Yet in every soul it lies,
A promise wrapped in moonlit gain.

So chase the mirage's glow,
Embrace the magic, let it stream,
For in this dance, we come to know,
The truth revealed in gossamer dreams.

Luminous Reflections in a Fog

Within the fog, a lantern shines,
Illumined paths of silver light,
The world transformed in blurred lines,
Where shadows waltz with the night.

Soft echoes whisper tales untold,
Of journeys etched in twilight's lace,
In this haven, brave and bold,
We seek the warmth of a gentle embrace.

Luminous glimmers in the air,
A dance of prisms, quiet grace,
Each heartbeat a tale to share,
Where dreams and reality interlace.

Reflections ripple, secrets yearn,
In the mist, a story is spun,
With every flicker, hearts discern,
The promise of a new day begun.

So roam these realms, with eyes wide,
For magic breeds in the unseen,
In luminous reflections, we glide,
Through the fog, to the breaking scene.

Celestial Secrets Under Shrouded Skies

Beneath the cloak of midnight's grace,
Stars hide their stories, dense and deep,
In silence, secrets leave no trace,
Whispers in the cosmos softly creep.

Moonlit paths, in shadows cast,
A tapestry of dreams entwined,
Invisible threads, a spell is vast,
Connecting hearts and fates aligned.

In the stillness, echoes chime,
Celestial voices call us near,
To dance with time, to write in rhyme,
The mysteries only few can hear.

Thus in the dark, we seek to find,
Each star a hope, a silent cry,
Unraveling the cosmic mind,
Under shrouded yet watchful skies.

So let us wander, hand in hand,
Emblazoned dreams that softly rise,
For in the quiet, we understand,
The celestial secrets in disguise.

Dusk's Embrace in Mystic Realms

As twilight drapes the evening veil,
Mystic realms begin to unfurl,
With echoes of a fairy's tale,
In colors soft that swirl and whirl.

Dusk's embrace, a tender sigh,
The horizon blurs, a gentle kiss,
Between the worlds where shadows lie,
Awaits a dream spun from pure bliss.

In twilight's glow, we find our fate,
Where wishes linger in the breeze,
A bridge between the small and great,
In magic, life begins to tease.

Through glades of wonder, spirits roam,
Each footfall sings the night's refrain,
In mystic realms, we find our home,
Where every heart can know no pain.

So gather round as night unfolds,
Embrace the quiet, treasure dreams,
For in dusk's arms, life gently molds,
A symphony of starlit themes.

Shimmering Traces of Twilight Hues

In the hush of dusk so sweet,
Whispers of day begin to fleet.
Stars awaken, soft and bright,
Painting dreams in the velvet night.

Crimson and gold in a dance so fair,
Embers linger in the cooling air.
Silhouettes of trees take flight,
Guardians of the fading light.

Moonlit paths through shadows wend,
Mysteries weave, as echoes blend.
Glimmers of hope in the dark's embrace,
Twilight reveals magic's face.

Night's perfume cloaks the land,
Gentle hush where dreams expand.
Twinkling lights, like fireflies soar,
In whispers soft, they beckon more.

Each star a tale, an ancient song,
Guiding lost souls who wander long.
With shimmering traces, the night shall rise,
A tapestry spun in the twilight skies.

Sylvan Phantoms in Waning Light

In the woods where shadows creep,
Sylvan phantoms begin to leap.
They dance on paths of fallen leaves,
In twilight's glow, the heart believes.

Whispers weave through branches bare,
Carrying secrets in the air.
Misty forms in the fading blaze,
Shimmer like stars in hidden ways.

Through thickets deep, the soft winds play,
Carrying scents of night and day.
Echoes of laughter, soft and shy,
In the realms where the quiet sigh.

With every rustle, a tale unfolds,
Of dreams and longings, the forest holds.
In waning light, the magic grows,
As the heart awakens to what it knows.

Bathed in twilight, the phantoms sway,
Dancing freely till break of day.
In their embrace, the spirit flies,
In sylvan dreams where hope never dies.

Lullabies of Shadows and Smoke

Under the blanket of evening's shroud,
Whispers of secrets, soft yet loud.
The shadows stretch, their stories told,
In cities hushed, in realms of gold.

Sooty tendrils rise and twist,
Crafting tales of those missed.
Each sigh, a promise, each breath, a song,
In the choir of night, where all belong.

Embers glow in the muted dark,
Guiding lost souls with a spark.
The lullabies call in the still of night,
Wrapping weary hearts in gentle light.

Through alleys narrow, and fears untold,
The smoke reveals what the heart holds.
In darkened corners, dreams awake,
With each new dawn, fresh paths to take.

Rise with the sun, with shadows blend,
As day unfolds, let old tales mend.
For in the echoes of night's soft stroke,
Lie lullabies of shadows and smoke.

Faint Glimmers Under the Gloom

In the corners where dark hours dwell,
Faint glimmers weave a secret spell.
Lost in the moments, time's gentle sweep,
Sleepers of shadows begin to leap.

Through thickened air, like phantom light,
Glimmers chase the edge of night.
A dance of hope, fragile yet bold,
Whispering tales that yearn to be told.

In the silent heart of the slumbering grove,
Faint sparks of magic, the soul's cove.
Under the gloom where fears may hide,
Stars still twinkle, a hopeful guide.

Each flicker brightens the path ahead,
Promising warmth where once there was dread.
In twilight's embrace, the shadows play,
Reminding us all, dawn brings a new day.

With every pulse of the dreaming earth,
Glimmers rise to celebrate rebirth.
In the depths of night, we find our room,
To dance with the stars, beyond all gloom.

Dreamscapes of the Veiled Enchantment

In whispers soft, the night unfolds,
Where starlit dreams weave tales of old.
Beneath the moon's enchanted gaze,
Time drifts like mist in silvery haze.

Through hidden paths where shadows play,
A world emerges, bright as day.
With each step taken, secrets sprout,
In magic realms where hearts scream out.

The air vibrates with gentle sighs,
As faeries dance beneath the skies.
They twirl through dreams both bold and bright,
Painting wishes in the night.

Cloaked in veils of twinkling light,
With every heartbeat, pure delight.
They beckon souls with laughter sweet,
In this enchanted, hallowed street.

So close your eyes, let spirits soar,
As dreamscapes open every door.
Through veiled enchantments, find your way,
And magic lingers, come what may.

Chasing Shadows Through Glistening Veils

In misty realms where secrets dwell,
The shadows weave their haunting spell.
With glistening veils, they softly glide,
Inviting you to take a ride.

Through whispering woods, the phantoms sigh,
Each step inviting, asking why.
They dance among the trees so grand,
In twilight's arms, hand in hand.

Their laughter echoes, sweet and low,
As time drifts softly, to and fro.
In shimmering light, the shadows blend,
A tapestry that knows no end.

Chasing dreams on silver streams,
Through glistening veils, the heart redeems.
In every ray, a story spins,
As mystery waltzes and begins.

So follow where the shadows lead,
In enchanted paths, your heart is freed.
With every heartbeat, feel the thrill,
Chasing shadows, time stands still.

Melodies of the Hidden Sylphs

In twilight's hush, the sylphs arise,
Their whispers weave like lullabies.
With notes that shimmer, soft and clear,
They fill the night with magic near.

Through moonlit woods, their voices soar,
A symphony of ancient lore.
With every breeze, a tale untold,
In hidden glades where dreams unfold.

Their laughter spills like silver streams,
A melody spun from twilight dreams.
In dappling light, they flit and dart,
Enchanting every watching heart.

Among the flowers, gently swaying,
The sylphs enchant with songs they're playing.
Their rhythms dance on fragrant air,
A magic song beyond compare.

So linger long, let melodies bind,
Two worlds as one, the heart aligned.
In whispers soft, their secrets blend,
The sylphs' sweet song shall never end.

Fantasia Wrapped in Whispering Gloom

In shadows deep, a tale takes flight,
Fantasia clings to the edge of night.
Wrapped in gloom, a world unfolds,
Where every dream a mystery holds.

Beneath the stars, the whispers surge,
As magic pulses with a quiet urge.
Through velvet dark, the secrets weave,
And beckon those who dare believe.

In shimmering teardrops, memories gleam,
Caught in the fabric of whispered dreams.
A dance of shadows, soft and light,
In the eerie hush of velvet night.

Through twisted paths where echoes loom,
The heart finds solace in whispered gloom.
Each breath a promise, each sigh a chance,
In this enchanted, timeless dance.

So step into the twilight's embrace,
Where dreams await in this haunted space.
In fantasia, the soul takes flight,
Wrapped in the magic of endless night.

Shadows Cradling Elfin Dreams

In twilight's hush, the shadows play,
Where elfin whispers softly sway.
Dancing lights in the evening mist,
A secret world, too sweet to resist.

They weave their songs of ancient lore,
Through hidden glades and enchanted door.
With every breeze, a tale unfurls,
A symphony of magic swirls.

In silver strands of starlit threads,
The dreams of elves like rivers spread.
Cradled close, they softly gleam,
Awakening hope in a night's serene.

With every heartbeat, soft and slow,
The shadows cradle dreams that grow.
In moonbeam light, they take their flight,
Elfin wonders hidden from sight.

So let your heart, in silence bound,
Embrace the love that knows no ground.
For in this realm, where dreams unfold,
The shadows keep what's true and bold.

Tales Spun in Moonlit Fog

Within the fog, where secrets lie,
Tales spiral up to the velvet sky.
Whispers of magic, soft and light,
In the embrace of the silvery night.

Figures dance in the glow of dreams,
Carving their fates in moonlit streams.
Each story wrapped in a gossamer thread,
Woven pathways where few have tread.

Silver faeries flit with glee,
Casting spells for all to see.
With laughter bright through the fog they glide,
Where enchantment waits, and fears subside.

The night unfolds, a canvas wide,
Cloaked in mysteries, we may abide.
In the tender kiss of soft moonlight,
The tales of old come alive in flight.

So linger long, let your heart believe,
In the moon's embrace, there's much to weave.
For every whisper the night may bring,
Holds the power of dreams to sing.

Veil of the Lost and Found

Beneath the veil of whispering trees,
Echoes linger on every breeze.
Lost memories dance in the twilight's glow,
Where the heart seeks what it longs to know.

In twilight's arms, the forgotten roam,
Searching for hints of a vanished home.
Each fragment glimmers like dew on grass,
In the stillness, their stories pass.

Curled in shadows, the lost take flight,
Haunting the edges of fading light.
With every step, a path reclaims,
The embers of life, now soft like flames.

Through ancient corners, echoes arise,
Carrying whispers of faded skies.
The veil of time, both cruel and kind,
Holds treasures within for those who find.

So let the wanderers seek their peace,
In the quiet moments, may heartaches cease.
For what is lost may still be found,
Beneath the veil where love's unbound.

Faint Echoes Under the Willow's Weep

Under the willow's gentle weep,
Faint echoes of memories softly creep.
Where shadows linger by a silver stream,
The past unfurls like a whispered dream.

Branches sway with a tender grace,
Holding secrets, time can't erase.
In every rustle, a tale is spun,
Of lovers lost, and battles won.

Softly sighs the evening breeze,
Carrying stories with effortless ease.
Underneath the stars that gleam,
Hides the heart of an ancient theme.

In twilight hours, where silence reigns,
Faint echoes linger, haunting the plains.
Through the whispers of the willow's embrace,
Time stands still in this sacred space.

So sit awhile, let your spirit soar,
In the echoes that dance forevermore.
For beneath the willow, life intertwines,
With every heartbeat, love enshrines.

Curfew of the Enchanted Veil

In twilight hours, when shadows creep,
The veil descends, secrets to keep.
Whispers caress the dappled ground,
As magic swirls, all around.

Fairy lights in the distance gleam,
Beneath the stars, we softly dream.
With every breath, the world feels whole,
A gentle pull on the heart and soul.

The clock strikes ten, the night's embrace,
A fleeting moment, a timeless space.
Underneath the moon's soft glow,
The enchanted veil conceals the flow.

Each creature stirs, in slumber's song,
In sacred woods, where we belong.
Curfew falls, the night winds sigh,
While echoes of laughter bid goodbye.

As dawn approaches, shadows fade,
The magic sleeps, safe in the glade.
A promise whispered, soft and light,
Until the next enchanted night.

Reverent Dreams of the Enigmatic

In realms where stars weave tales untold,
The mysteries of time unfold.
Reverent dreams, like rivers flow,
In secret gardens, we learn and grow.

Faceless spirits in the moon's embrace,
Guide wandering hearts through this sacred space.
Echoes of laughter, sweet melodies,
Dance through the air on gentle breeze.

Awake the magic of night's caress,
In the silence, we sense the blessed.
A flicker of hope among ancient trees,
In whispers of lore, our souls find ease.

The enigmatic calls, will you abide?
In the tapestry woven, where shadows reside.
Each thread a story, each color a truth,
In reverent dreams, we reclaim our youth.

With every heartbeat, a spell renews,
In twilight's glow, we become the muse.
In this enchanted dance, we hear the song,
Of worlds beyond, where we belong.

Smoke and Mirrors in the Fae Wilderness

In the woods where illusions play,
Smoke and mirrors guide the way.
Each flicker of light, a tale begins,
In the heart of shadows, the magic spins.

Glimmers of truth, shrouded in mist,
Secrets and sighs that cannot be missed.
Fae whispers sweet, like honeyed wine,
In tangled branches, we wish to entwine.

A tapestry woven with dreams unseen,
In the depths of the wild, where echoes glean.
A flutter of wings, a shimmer of dust,
In the air, we feel the ancient trust.

Through the labyrinth of time and fate,
The fae wilderness beckons, we contemplate.
With every step, a choice unfolds,
In smoke and mirrors, the truth upholds.

From dusk till dawn, a playful dance,
In the wild, we lose ourselves in chance.
With laughter and joy, the fae twirl about,
In the world of magic, there's never a doubt.

Glassy Eyes of Woodland Sorrow

In the hush of woods where shadows dwell,
Glassy eyes hold stories to tell.
Beneath the branches, whispers sigh,
Echoes of loss, as the moments die.

Every tear that falls like rain,
Carves a path through heart's deep pain.
Lost in the silence, the spirits cry,
For all that was, and all that'll die.

Nature weeps, her beauty fades,
In every grove, the memory wades.
Yet through the sorrow, hope can bloom,
From ashes of grief, life finds room.

A flicker of light in the darkest night,
Glimmers of hope in lost human plight.
With resilience found in the heart of the wood,
In tales of sorrow, we rise as we should.

Among the trees, through pain we grow,
With glassy eyes, we learn to show,
That even in sorrow, love can reside,
In the woodland's heart, our tears collide.

Arcane Tales on Shimmering Winds

Beneath the stars, the whispers weave,
Old enchantments dance, and shadows believe.
A tapestry spun from the twilight's loom,
Secrets of magic in every bloom.

The breeze entwines with silken threads,
Echoes of legends where light softly spreads.
In the heart of the night, the tales do reside,
Balancing dreams on a gossamer tide.

Wraiths of forgotten, in silence they glide,
Carrying hopes where the lost ones abide.
Through the moonlit skies, their stories take flight,
Arcane realms shining with brilliance so bright.

Glimmers of wisdom in ancient tomes,
In the cool, gentle night, the enchantment roams.
Through images woven with longing and grace,
Lost in the beauty of this hallowed space.

So listen closely, and heed the call,
For in the shimmering winds, there's magic for all.
An echo of laughter that dances on high,
In the arcane tales where the lost spirits sigh.

Whirls of Enchantment in Mysterious Woods

In the forest deep, where shadows creep,
Glowing lights twinkle, secrets they keep.
Whispers of faeries in the cool night air,
Dancing in circles, a magical fare.

Gnarled branches twist in twilight's embrace,
Every rustle a story, in this sacred space.
The moon hangs low, a sentinel bright,
Guarding the wonders unleashed by the night.

Footsteps of adventurers, past and present,
Finding the path where the lost are but pleasant.
The air thick with laughter, the sweet scent of pine,
Entwined with enchantments, both yours and divine.

Violet petals underfoot softly sigh,
Each whispering story, a reason to fly.
In this realm of wonder, dreams breathe anew,
Where mystery lingers, and magic shines through.

So lose yourself among the trees,
And follow the melody carried by the breeze.
For in whirls of enchantment, your heart shall find,
The beauty of worlds where wonder is blind.

Ghostly Embers of Forgotten Lore

Amidst the ruins, shadows flicker bright,
Ghostly embers ignite the night.
Echoes of whispers, long silenced by time,
Haunting the air with a spectral rhyme.

Old stories linger where the past holds ground,
In every crack and creak, wise knowledge is found.
Fables unraveled in the moon's soft glow,
Breath of the ancients, in twilight's flow.

Step carefully, dear heart, through this tale,
Where souls linger close; their voices prevail.
Long-forgotten heroes, now shadows and sighs,
Guide us to truths in the darkening skies.

With every flicker, a memory stirs,
The dance of the ages in silence occurs.
Let the warmth of their fire ignite your own flame,
In ghostly embers, we whisper their name.

So gather round, and listen with care,
For lore is alive in the specter-laden air.
As the night enfolds, let the stories restore,
The magic of ages in forgotten lore.

Flickering Lights in the Enchanted Gloom

In the heart of the dark, where shadows entwine,
Flickering lights in the dusk offer sign.
Ghosts of the past in merriment play,
Guiding lost wanderers who've lost their way.

Beneath the twisted boughs, magic ignites,
In every shimmering glimmer, enchantment invites.
The whisper of breezes, a haunting refrain,
Weaving through spirits that linger like rain.

What secrets are held in this luminous haze,
Where time bends softly in a mystical daze?
Lost tales of love and a promise that soared,
In flickering lights, their hearts were restored.

Crickets sing sweetly, the night is alive,
In cozy corners, where shadows arrive.
Glimmers of wonder in the hush of the night,
Creating a symphony of spectral delight.

So follow the lights, let them guide your heart,
Through enchanted gloom, where the shadows depart.
For magic awaits in the fluttering gleam,
A world deep with wonder, a luminous dream.

The Hazy Requiem of the Night

In moonlit whispers, secrets soar,
The shadows dance on the polished floor.
A lullaby drifts through velvet skies,
As dreams and echoes softly rise.

Wanderers tread on paths of grey,
Where stars conceal their bright display.
Each heartbeat murmurs of things unseen,
In twilight's fold, where night has been.

A ghostly tune calls forth the brave,
From crumbling stones by the darkened wave.
The nightingale sings, full of despair,
In the stillness, whispers drift through air.

Yet dawn's soft light begins to blush,
Bringing calm to the starry hush.
With laughter ringing through the vale,
And hopes reborn in morning's tale.

The requiem fades with the morning's gleam,
As life awakes from a fleeting dream.
In the hush of night, a promise lies,
In every shadow, a tale that sighs.

Serpentine Shadows on Moonlit Glades

Whispers of twilight, they slither and sway,
Through fern-clad paths where wild creatures play.
Serpentine shadows weave tales of old,
In glades of silver, where secrets are told.

The willows dance, with leaves that gleam,
Beneath the moonlight's silken beam.
Each brush of wind tells a tale anew,
Of wanderers lost, and journeys true.

Flickering lanterns dot the dew-kissed ground,
With every flicker, a magic is found.
The earth and sky in harmony meet,
In this enchanted realm, where dreams repeat.

Murmurs of longing in the cool night air,
Secrets that spirits and shadows share.
An owl's soft call breaks the velvety calm,
A haunting reminder of nature's balm.

As dawn sneaks in with a golden gaze,
The shadows retreat, as light starts to blaze.
In the heart of the night, wonders abide,
In the depths of the glades, where dreams coincide.

The Crystal Grotto's Breath

In caverns deep where echoes dwell,
A crystal grotto weaves its spell.
Icicle chandeliers shimmer and glow,
Reflecting tales of long ago.

The silken whispers of ancient streams,
Flow secrets wrapped in shimmering dreams.
Each drop of water sings its song,
In this enchanted world where shadows belong.

Stalactites drape like curtains of lace,
In the stillness, time slows its pace.
A haven for wishes that drift like mist,
In twilight's embrace, sore hearts are kissed.

The gentle pulse of the grotto's breath,
Tells stories beyond life and death.
With every heartbeat, the darkness sways,
In sparkling light, the sorrow decays.

But as dawn approaches, the magic fades,
The crystals dim, retreat into shades.
Yet in each echo, the memories cling,
Of a hidden world where the heart can sing.

Fables Bound in a Misty Sphere

In the morning mist, where shadows reside,
Fables are whispered, where dreams coincide.
Each tale unfurls like a tapestry spun,
In a world of magic, where wonders run.

The fae gather 'neath the ancient boughs,
In hidden realms, their solemn vows.
With laughter and song that twirls in the air,
They weave their stories with utmost care.

With every sunrise, new legends arise,
Bound in the mists that cloak the skies.
Each whispering leaf tells stories profound,
In the hush of a sphere where lost truths are found.

The echoes of history dance on the breeze,
In harmony, time flows with ease.
A tapestry woven from threads of fate,
Among the glimmers where shadows await.

And as twilight wraps the world in its shawl,
The verses of night heed the ancients' call.
In fables bound by a misty sphere,
The heart finds its tale, the soul finds its cheer.

A Dance with the Unseen

In shadows deep, where silence sways,
The flicker of fate in moonlit haze.
Whirls of magic, a gentle breeze,
Twist through the night with whispered pleas.

A partner sought in twilight's glow,
Shifting shapes in the ebb and flow.
Hands entwined with breath so light,
Together we sway in the still of night.

Vows unspoken drift on air,
With each heartbeat, we dance with care.
Eyes closed tight, the world ignites,
In the echo of stars, we find our sights.

The rhythm of life, a tender tease,
Guided softly by unseen keys.
With every spin, the shadows play,
A dance with dreams that will not stay.

Yet in the dawn, the veil will break,
And we shall part for morning's sake.
But memories swirl on the edge of day,
A lingering waltz, forever to stay.

Enigmatic Veils of the Ether

Beneath the fabric of the night,
Lies a mystery cloaked in light.
Whispers pass through a gauzy shroud,
Secrets stitched with threads of cloud.

Each star a dream, each moonbeam cast,
Echoes of futures, shadows of past.
Winds carry tales from realms unseen,
As the universe hums a tranquil theme.

In twilight's hush, the veils will sway,
Guiding lost souls who wander and play.
They dance upon the zephyrs' rise,
Cloaked in mystery 'neath silver skies.

Time bends softly in ethereal flow,
Where pathways cross, and spirits glow.
A realm where wishes are gently spun,
Weaving wonders 'til night is done.

So reach within your heart's embrace,
For the unseen is a sacred space.
In the dance of light, we shall confide,
In enigmatic veils, where secrets abide.

Whispers of Lore in a Dappled Glade

In a glade where shadows twine,
Whispers weave through branches fine.
Stories echo, both old and wise,
Nestled deep where the heart lies.

Beneath the boughs, a tale takes flight,
Voices linger in the soft twilight.
A touch of wonder, a hint of grace,
In that sacred, nature-kissed place.

Mossy stones hold centuries' sighs,
As the gentle breeze carries lullabies.
Each leaf a page of forgotten lore,
Awaiting the seeker who longs for more.

Sunlight dapples the forest floor,
As dreams unfurl and spirits soar.
In laughter shared and secrets told,
The glade holds treasures worth more than gold.

So come, dear wanderer, heed the call,
For the whispers await, a timeless thrall.
In every rustle, in every shade,
Find the magic that spirits have made.

Dreams Adrift in Celestial Smoke

In the realm where stardust flows,
Dreams are stitched as twilight glows.
Floating softly on the cosmic tide,
In celestial smoke, our hopes abide.

Visions shimmer in the silver night,
Each breath a promise, a flickering light.
We sail through realms of endless sky,
As constellations whisper 'goodbye'.

Past the planets, in the velvet deep,
Ghostly echoes cradle sleep.
A world where wishes learn to soar,
Every sigh opens a new door.

In the embrace of a cosmic dream,
Reality fades, all is as it seems.
Held by the threads of a softest smoke,
Where every heartbeat becomes a cloak.

So close your eyes, drift gently past,
In this sacred void, free from the vast.
For dreams adrift, like stars will gleam,
In the tender glow of a timeless dream.